To
Kerry (You missed a treat)

Thankyou

ISBN: 9798373074155

KDP Independent Publishing

Some Words, In an Order, On a Page.

By Ryan Kenny

Some Words, In an Order, On a Page.

Chapter 1: The beginning part of a book.

I have been told that most books require an introduction or some kind of reference to what the book is about. So, this is it.

It's a poetry book.

If you do not like poetry I understand, I don't either. However, I do highly recommend that you read it. Just pretend that you are reading slow songs without a beat, or even approach it with the same intrigue as you would if you found an abandoned shopping list on the floor of the local Morrison's.

Here is a shopping list I found:

-Bananas

-Meat for Tuesday

-Pasta, any shape

-Burgers + barms

-Satsumas

-Tissues

-£40 for John

(I often wonder if John got his money)

Poem #3

Sweat poured down Gillian's face,
Her heart pounded as she reached the last metres of the 26 miles.
She was in the lead,
She must have been.
There was no one else in sight,
There was no one…

Maybe she had got the date of the marathon wrong.

Gillian walked home.

Fucking shattered.

This page was left intentionally blank.

Poem #149

Thomason and his large family were sat in a giant circle on the grass.

"Let's play a game!" Thomason's son suggested,

"Duck, Duck, Goose?" Thomason said getting some enthusiastic nods from the party.

So, they played.

Duck.
Duck.
Duck.
Duck.
Duck.
Duck.
GOOSE!

Thomason ran into the nearby lake pursued by his six-year-old daughter,

He swam and swam, and the poor girl could never catch him.

The police were called.

Thomason was reported as a missing person.

That was ten years ago now.

Poem #21*

There was no more bamboo at the zoo,
The keepers had no idea what to do.
The Pandas were livid,
Their anger was vivid,
So, the Zookeepers shot them dead.

*This is one of the very few poems that rhyme, so if that's the kind of thing you are into, I am glad to have tickled your delights.

Ryan Kenny
Poem #18

Gregory walked into Starbucks.

"Give me some of that green tea!" Gregory whispered loudly to one of the customers who was clearly drinking a cappuccino.

Gregory heaved the cup away from her frothy mouth and took an almighty sip,

Then he left,

Exclaiming that green tea tastes a lot like cappuccino.

Some Words, In an Order, On a Page.

Chapter 2: Holidays

All these poems were written on holiday.

It was a wonderful trip to Lanzarote full of the best three things in life: Food, sun and endless people watching. I do apologise for the next sentence because this is a massive pet peeve of mine within stand up…

…But this next bit actually happened…

Me and my newest Wife had booked the same hotel as we had the previous years because we absolutely hate change. It was coincidently our 5th time to that part of Lanzarote because as I say, I don't do different. On arrival we marched into the lobby as any sane person would after getting off the limbo that is an airport transfer. The lobby was closed. Paint pots glinted in the dim flickering lights and a finger tapped us on the shoulder.

A Spanish security guard angrily pointed across the road to a different hotel, we had essentially been Mary'd and Joseph'd, if the inns in the nativity were under refurbishment instead of just full.

To cut a long story short we stayed in wonderful hotel and had a great time.

But we felt icky all holiday.

Because of change. I DON'T DO CHANGE.

<u>Poem #98</u>

A two-penny piece lay alone and unclaimed at gate A11 of
terminal 2,
There were plenty of people around.
An old man stared at it for a while,
Before being ushered away by his wife.
There was a cost-of-living crisis,
And yet this penny lay unloved.
So, I waited,
Until everyone boarded their flight.
Then I snapped it up,
2p richer I thought.
As I looked to see if there were any tickets available on the
next flight.

Poem #74

A queue of people stood queuing at the gate,

Whilst those who thought they knew better sat spread out on the plastic seats.

Not one of them knew if they had made the right decision,

Apart from the guy at the desk,

Who muttered nonsense into the tannoy about tickets between seats 14 and 16.

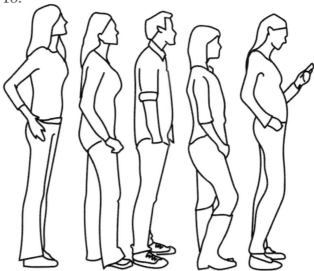

<u>Poem #42</u>

The plane took off,
He sucked on his foxes glacier mint,
Prematurely.
So, he had another,
His breath minty fresh but ears still painful as hell,
Those at the foxes glacier mint head office laughing their
sticky hands off!

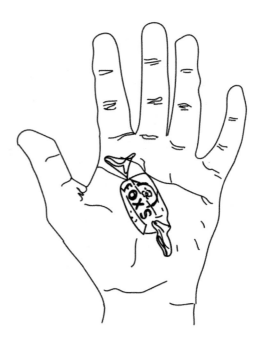

Ryan Kenny
<u>Poem #41</u>

The man was stuck behind the concessions trolley,
Everyman and his dog wanted hot chocolate or minstrels,
which the stewardess kept in the draw at the bottom.
He kept pulling faces to his Mrs,
To try and make light of the situation.
But inside he was seething,
"There really should be a layby on this stupid plane".
He thought to himself,
Still stuck.

<u>Poem #13</u>

With every pull another sheet was removed,
Each one a lot tighter than the one before.
It took himself, his wife, a housecleaner and a Scottish bloke
they had made friends with 2 hours to remove the final sheet.
The bed was finally accessible,
So, politely he asked them all to join him in it for a snooze.

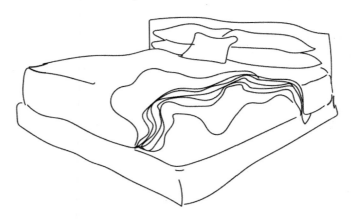

Poem #108

Mr Tompkins was stood at the pool bar,
He was practising his Spanish under his breath.
"Un vino por favour" he had meant to say.
But instead,
Shouted,
"BIBLIOTECA," as loud as he could.

He walked back to the table without the wine,
But he now owned a library,
Which was nice.

Poem #73

Rafael Nadal served for the 80th time that game,
It was a slow serve, so he had a few moments to think.
It was all so pointless,
The endless swings.

He returned the ball over the net

He could be finishing his air fix,
Or checking on the lasagne he had left in the Wimbledon ovens.

He returned the ball again feigning a grunt for the crowd

He remembered a sweet memory of his old nan, who used to pick olives on the farm,
Those days were so simple.

He lost the game,
Should have been concentrating.

Poem #85

8 Dads got into the lift,

The colourful cornucopia of rarely used beach towels wrapped tightly under their arms.

One had towel pegs which immediately made him the alpha.

The one with the football tattoo on his burnt shoulder spoke first,

"We have to get there before the Germans don't we," he joked.

They all looked at him,

Took out their German-to-English mini translator pocketbooks,

And beat him to death with them.

Poem #126

The new intake had arrived,
Clueless to the ways of the hotel.
Us old timers knew the secrets,
But we wouldn't want to give away our buffet optimisation techniques.
They didn't even know there was a pool table with a dodgy pocket in the room next to the lobby,
They also had no idea where the screaming children like to congregate or the name of the lovely bar person who secretly turned singles into doubles.
We looked at them like scum,
They looked at our burnt faces and waved.
"Sorry mate we've already made our holiday friends," we said internally.
They had so much to learn, they didn't even know the aircon didn't work when the balcony door was open.

Oh, how we envied them.

Chapter 3: Not holidays.

Thank you for making it this far, I am sure you are having one hell of a time. Also, apologies for some of the language in this book. If you are reading to a small child or a prune, then I suggested bleeping out those words. Failing that, double down on it and just read those words out even louder, they will soon learn to respect you.

<u>Poem #136</u>

The four nurses from the x-ray room liked to x-ray random things to alleviate the stresses of the day. They x-rayed an apple on Friday,
    A stapler on Saturday,
    And a sand wedge on Sunday.

None of which had bones,
But they had fun.

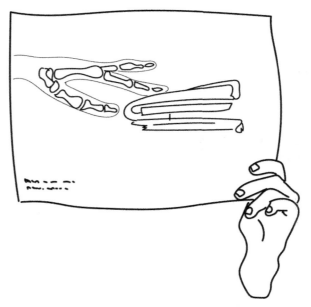

Ryan Kenny
Poem #6

No one wanted to be first to the buffet,
They all waited as the once hot food began to chill.
The catering staff left hours ago,
It was the flies that arrived first,
Followed inevitably by the maggots.
The smell was unbearable.
But still they sat,
Stubborn and dead.

mmm delicious!

<u>Poem #75</u>

Not really a poem but what is.

In the early 50s, Yewar Gully-Bull, a scientist from South Africa discovered that paper has a much higher odour retention rate than most materials. However, due to more pressing concerns these discoveries have been rarely used in our day-to-day lives.

Its only surviving use is the scratch and sniff.

So, to honour him I have imprinted a fragrance on this page. (I do hope it doesn't spread to adjacent pages, but this can happen).

Take a few long sniffs and try and work out the fragrance.

Ask your mates/family/guardian if they agree with your smell.

The answer is on page 65.

Poem #120

It was 19:58.
Ian was stood by his confectionary cupboard,
Dancing on his tippy toes like an excited toddler.

It was 19:59.
The sweat poured down his brow,
He and the entire twitch stream had been waiting for this moment for almost 24 hours.

It was 20:00.
He swung open the door and removed the sweet goodness from its ineffective sheath,
Then proceeded to munch on the packet of thin dark mints.

It was 20:00:14
His husband walked in,
"You do know the clocks went back last night, don't you?"

It was 20:00:19
Ian spat the After 8's into his sweetheart's open palm and sobbed.

Poem #46

The planets sat in their galaxy conference room,
Kepler 22B from HR walked in and gave them a look that made Saturn's rings tighten.
Kepler, who needed to be brought in from another galaxy, handed out leaflets on diversity and inclusion.
Venus looked at mercury, fire in her eyes,
Uranus shat himself,
Neptune went pale, Mars bright red.

Kepler tutted.

"There have been complaints from an individual regarding unfair dismissal", Kepler said.
Everyone looked at Earth,
The xenophobic bastard.

"You cannot just dismiss someone because they are a dwarf."

Ryan Kenny

Poem #137

The Kernel was raging,
He was hot with anger.
He began to shake,
The fury almost burning him.

And then he popped,
And the other soldiers ate him.

Poem #147

Every single snooker referee in the Crucible fell ill with a poisoning that could be tracked back to the canteen,
The players decided to ref the games themselves.
It started quite civil at first,
The next players even began to place pound coins on the table.
But by the quarter final everything had gone to shit,
Ronnie O'Sullivan placed cups in the pockets,
And Hendry smirred chalk across Graham Dott's shiny head.
The Semis were even worse,
Judd Trump filled his little water jug with smarties,
And Robertson smirred more chalk across Graham Dott's shiny head.
Graham Dott got knocked out in the first round,
It just felt like bullying by that point.

Ronnie O'Sullivan won.

Chapter 4: Poems from The Heart.

A lot of poets can write perfect prose describing their inner thoughts.

Maya Angelou:
They dull my eyes, yet
I keep on dying,
Because I love to live.

William Wordsworth:
Do I behold these steep and lofty cliffs,
That on a wild secluded scene impress
Thoughts of more deep seclusion; and connect
The landscape with the quiet of the sky.

Richard Aldington:
The bitterness.
 the misery, the wretchedness of childhood
Put me out of love with God.

Ryan Kenny:
The Pandas were livid,
Their anger was vivid,
So, the Zookeepers shot them dead.

Poem #1

I find it quite hard to write meaningful poems,
It is most likely due to my talent in squashing most of my emotions.
If they are laughing,
They are not asking.
And if they are not asking,
Then I am not saying.

I find it quite hard to write meaningful poems.

Chapter 5: A bunch of Haikus

Haiku Poems are an ancient form of poem writing which is renowned for its small size as well as the precise punctuation and syllables needed on its three lines.

That being said…

Poem #77

An earthquake struck Stoke*,
Destroying the whole city,
Nobody noticed.

*Feel free to replace the place name with that of another single syllable, Hull, Bath, Crewe and Ayr all work in this case.

Poem #105

They span the wheel,
They won four months of energy,
The country is fucked.

Ryan Kenny

Poem #128

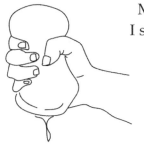

My sponge absorbed all,
I squeezed it over the sink,
Peter Falk fell out.

Poem #36

The elephant screamed,
A mouse ran under its feet,
And sliced its hamstrings.

Poem #145

Bought myself a shark,
To vanquish my enemies,
The wife was annoyed.

Chapter 6: A Trip to the Casino

All these poems are based in the confines of a casino, so if that is not that obvious from some of the poems, imagine the scene as you read.

I was in the confines of the casino when I wrote this entire chapter, I had just lost £10 on the roulette table so obviously I was in a delicate mind space. But I like to think I drunk £10 worth of Coke Zero and that I was, in fact, winning.

Obviously please gamble responsibly.

Even if the pressures of Ray Winstone or Chris Akabusi become stronger than that of the will of Sauron.

Poem #79

The croupier spun the ball,
It bounced around the wheel.
It landed in 21,
And 4,
And 2,
And 19.

It was a bloody
big ball.

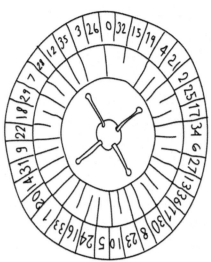

Ryan Kenny

Poem #80

I could not believe my luck,
I kept getting all the cards.
Everyone else was so jealous and angry with me,
Because I had stolen all their cards.

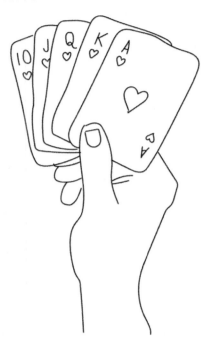

Poem #81

Craig was at the table,
Chips in his hands,
Vinegar drenching the King of Hearts.

Poem #82

Throbbing was a pack of cards inside Lucy's pocket,
She had bought them from a beach shop in Tenerife.
And now she couldn't wait to use them to win enough for another holiday,
She slipped two aces into her sleeve.
The dealer was initially amazed when Lucy revealed four red aces,
But became suspicious when two of the aces had various nude women in front of canary island landmarks adorning them.

They still paid out,
Because the dealer loved her personal cards.

Poem #83

Liam knew the system,
Whilst his friends pranced around the tables trying to 'do a rain man',
He ordered his 8th Coke Zero.

Liam, unlike his friends, left chuffed and in profit.
Until he got mugged,
And the damn criminal stole all his 8 Coke Zeros.

Ryan Kenny

Poem #84

Sixteen is red,
Twenty-four is black,

Dylan the croupier just had a heart attack.

Some Words, In an Order, On a Page.

Chapter 7: A few longer poems.

Sometimes poetry can be short and in other instances it can be long. Well in this chapter most of the poems are long. If you don't have a decent attention span, then I recommend you get a friend to read these poems out for you.

And if you don't have a friend,

Its probably because you read books,

NERD.

Poem #33

Nigel Hughes had a dilemma,
He could do something funny and entertaining for the sake of the poem.
Or he could he continue sitting on the bench,
Listening to his Louis Theroux documentary.

Two children played in the park,
One of them, the elder child, was springing up and down on one of those springy horses.
The younger child was on the floor,
Picking splinters out of his dry knees from the bark that the local council had considered the perfect substrate for hard landings.
And Nigel Hughes remained on the bench,
Oblivious and boring.

A young romantic couple were embraced in an argument that caused everyone to stare,
One of them pulled out a slingshot,
Whilst the other, clearly more prepared,
Signalled for a trebuchet to be dragged into play.
And still Nigel Hughes couldn't tear himself away from the audiobook.

Poem #89

Hundreds of kids jumped over one another for a bottle of Prime,
All trying to show off to their mates.
On lookers were bemused,
And commented how kids are "So ridiculous these days."
Adults rolled their eyes,
As the frenzy never ceased.
"Why are the kids of today so pathetic," one man said, who had a branded badge sown onto his jacket to make him look cool.
"You'll never see us acting so feral," a lady muttered, forgetting that she was the reason that Pogs were banned in here school.
At least you can drink Prime,
Unlike Pogs or fabric badges.

Poem #8

Two men stood under a lamppost,
Both getting drenched by the rain.
So, they decided to take turns,
Tom first,
Ben wet.
Ben next,
Tom wet.
Together,
Both wet.
Neither,
Both wet.
Ben on Tom,
Painful.
Tom on Ben,
Difficult.
Embraced,
Both dry.
Success,
Success.

Poem #40

Bang bang bang,
Go the drums.
Toot, toot, toot,
Go the flutes.
Swish, swish, swish,
Goes the conductors stick.
Violin noise, *violin noise*, *violin noise*,
Go the clarinets,
Completely out of tune.

Ryan Kenny

Poem #140

What's the best font for poetry?
This one?
Or this?
PEOPLE SAY THIS CAN WORK,
Others tend to suggest this.
But I like the classics,
And the hated.

Right, I have decided,
I have to be bold,
I know what font I would love to use for the rest of the book.

Poem #26

Liam had put too much duck on his pancake,
And it was a fucking car crash.
He hadn't left space for the stringy onions,
Or the ability to fold it.
Hoisin spilled all over his pathetic hands,
And incidentally,
His divorce papers.

He just couldn't do anything right.

Some Words, In an Order, On a Page.

Chapter 8: A few shorter poems

These poems are short.

<u>Poem #56</u>

The anaconda slithered onto the stage,
And gobbled Britney 'Bitch' Spears whole,
What a terrible idea.

#Fashion.

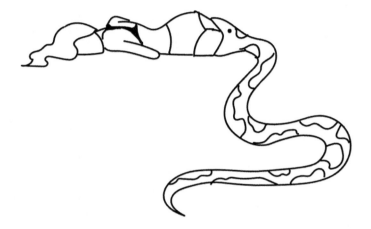

Poem #133

It took me 5 years to learn how to use chopsticks,
And finally.
After all that time,
I can announce.
I can now pick up a fork with chopsticks.

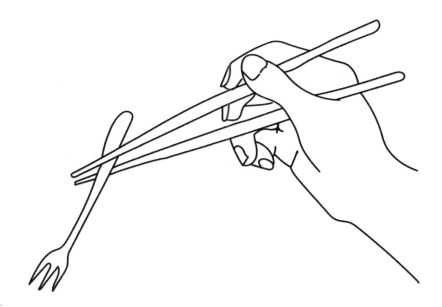

Poem #38

Scientists say that Jellyfish hold the secrets to eternal life,
But the greedy bastards just will not share.

Poem #44

A fire engine was called,
A great fire was raging.
Which was a completely inappropriate name for fire engine.

Poem #129

This isn't a haiku,
Although it may scan just like one,
Stop counting on your hands.

Poem #53

I was caught in a web of lies...

No sorry...

I was caught on a web with flies.

Some Words, In an Order, On a Page.

Chapter 9: Answers

Scratch and Sniff answer: Paper

Some Words, In an Order, On a Page.

Chapter 10: Poems I wrote on the 255 bus on the way to do a new material night.

The following chapter contains a bunch of poems that I wrote on the 255 bus. The bus itself goes from Partington to Manchester City centre.

Some of my favourite stops include:

Lodge Avenue: (Though as it's my local I maybe showing bias). There is a good view of a vintage car and its very close to an independent shop.

Trafford Bar: This is because the bus driver often uses this stop to catch up on his schedule to make sure he isn't early. It's good to get your own bearings at that time.

Bridgewater Hall: Depending on the time travelled you can sometimes see massive trucks unloading all sorts of musical equipment into the venue. I like the thought of the triangle player waiting around for his tiny case.

Piccadilly Gardens: It's the last stop and what's not to like.

Poem #60

The baby screamed and screamed,
Until I sung to them a sweet lullaby.
It nodded,
I was through to judge's houses.

Poem #61

Gordan Ramsey walked into a restaurant,
Everything was perfect,
They had a lovely time,

The end.

Poem #62

Tompkins turned to his wife,
"I don't like Prof. Brian Cox," he said.
His wife put down her fork, a half-eaten walls sausage trembling on its prongs,
She pointed at the door.
Tompkins left the house,
Ashamed of himself.
The smug northern bugger just confused him,
How could Tompkins enjoy a man that belittled him so much.
He walked into the familiar corridors of the rehab centre,
The receptionist giving him a wry smile and a knowing nod.
The centre will put him back on the straight and narrow,
He will learn to love the Professor again.

Ryan Kenny

Poem #63

After a trip to the cathedral tuck shop,
The Archbishop of Canterbury took off his giant hat.
Four Daim bars and a Fanta lemon fell out,
"Success," he whispered to himself in Latin.
He paused,
Looked around,
And took yet another lonely walk to the confessional booth.

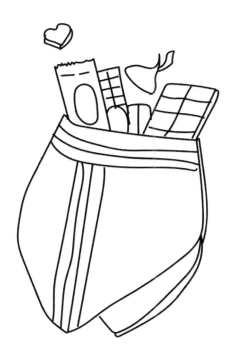

Poem #64

You are as busy as a bee,
As springy as a flea.
I have the same lifestyle as a manatee.

You are as wise as a bat,
As playful as a cat.
I am as useful to society as a biting gnat.

You are as loyal as an Alsatian,
As wanted as a dalmatian.
I am as boring as a rotten crustacean.

You are as precious as a lamb,
As strong as a ram.
I on the other hand, if you picked me up from my place of comfort, ripped me open and scooped out my insides, would die,
Just like a Clam.

Poem #65

"This fucker isn't paying us any rent," Grumpy said looking through last month's expenses.

"I hadn't noticed," Dopey squealed.

"We would have to each take up an extra shift in the mine," Doc suggested.

"Or we could kill the bitch?" Bashful muttered.

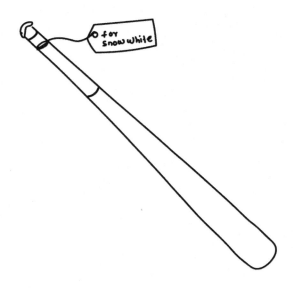

Chapter 11: The 8th best chapter

This is the 8th best chapter, feel free to rank the other chapters using this one as a measure. There are seven better chapters and a few not as good. I would be very interested in seeing your rankings so feel free to @ me or even email it me, my email can be made up using some of the letters within this book.

Poem #2

This is a poem by H.G Wells.

I never ask where do you go,
I never ask what do you do.
I never ever ask what's in your mind,
I never ever ask if you'll be mine.
Come and smile don't be shy,
Touch my bum this is life, oooooh.
We are the cheeky gi....

No sorry not HG Wells, it's by Chee-key Girls.

Ryan Kenny

Poem #114

Strikes eh,
Can't move in this country for endless strikes.
This morning a postal worker threw a rock through Trevor's
garage window,
And peered through,
A rail worker tried to knock down his door,
And a junior doctor tried to have him arrested,
So, he let them all out of his garage.

Poem #24

Napoleon looked around the battlefield,
Four young blondes were sat under a tree, taking notes.
One of them was tinkering with a grand piano,
Whilst another rummaged through a chest full of bright and colourful clothing.
Napoleon's blood boiled,
Which took fewer minutes to do than the other, taller generals.
"These twits better not be writing a song about this."

Poem #17

Wemby Jones had ambitions,
They wanted to stop smoking,
But they just couldn't.
They just couldn't stop masturbating to the images on the front of the packages.

Poem #110

Jamie Oliver sat on his baguette throne,
Nibble marks on the tips where he just couldn't help himself.
In front of him thousands of livestreams of primary school
canteens across the UK and Northern Ireland.
Not one Turkey Twizzler or Pasta King in sight,
A tear leaked from his beetroot face.
"I am completed," he said with a greasy, toothy smile,
And dissipated into a cloud of pink Himalayan rock salt.

<u>Poem #116</u>

A man, whose name is not important for the purposes of the poem,

Saw on TikTok that he had being going to the loo wrong his entire life.

Apparently, he learned,

He had to place his feet on a stool and raise his knees.

And not,

Shitting in the cistern whilst reading The New York Times.

Poem #30

Sue H reached for the official Collins dictionary once more,
"Aww come on Sue H, we don't need that, it's just a friendly game," her opponent tutted.
Sue H didn't even bother opening the fingered pages,
She stood and whacked her opponent over the head.
"How many time Carol, Qi is and acceptable word," she hissed,
Wiping the blood off her personal dictionary and strutting away.

<u>Poem #112</u>

They came in the droves,
Thousands of them.
They couldn't help themselves,
Falling over one another to get in
I saw them from my kitchen window,
I smirked.
I had opened the foil from the lid of my Yazoo,
My milkshake did bring them here.

Poem #96

The google calendar had just dropped,
Chuckles honked in frustration,
He was on carpool duty next week.
The alarm was set for 3am, Fiat Punto cleaned,
And he had imputed all 36 pick-up locations into his sat-nav.*

*I am fully aware that this is not my best work but the image of a clown carshare makes me chuckle. A slight chuckle at a thought is criteria enough to make this author include in.

<u>Poem #91</u>

A fluffy cat waited in the box,
Eager to surprise its owner,
Dr Schrodinger.

The cat pounced out,
Claws retracted and eyes full of kitten like hope.

Dr Schrodinger shot it,
Then wiped the blood off his apron,
And placed another tally mark in the 'dead cat' column on his whiteboard.

#Science

Poem #51

Two   ducks
waddled together in
a mucky pond.

"Quack, quack,"
the bigger duck said
to the other,
His feathery arms
going   like   the
clappers.

"QUACK QUACK," he said again, much more irate than
normal.
The little duck squinted,
"I can't fucking understand you mate!" He said angrily.

Poem #57

Uri Geller arose out of his metal cocoon,
His spoon cocoon.
His was crazy man in his spoon cocoon,
A loon in a spoon cocoon.
He would leave so rarely,
In a blue moon the loon would leave his spoon cocoon,
Which really annoyed his wife.

Chapter 12: The Zoo

I recently visited a zoo. It was a wonderful experience, so I decided to write a bunch of poems about what I witnessed. There may be some stretching of the truth, but I hope you can forgive me in that regard.

I will leave you to guess which zoo I visited from the sights and animals mentioned. I may even include the names of some of the animals though others have been changed to protect the identity of some of the residents

Poem #48

We had decided to watch the sea lion show,
There were 3 performances that day so naturally we planned our entire visit round them.
The 10:30 show would be full of the cockiest sea lions, and we didn't fancy that,
Whilst the 16:30 would be jammed packed full of guests who just couldn't organise themselves properly.
So, we elected for the 12:30 time,
A good time for a sea lion show I remember saying to the wife at the time.
It was as expected,
They didn't do anything truly impressive like file my taxes or solve the toxic debate around fracking.
Instead, they just patted balls and swam a bit,
Which got wondrous applause from the gullible mob surrounding them.
How easily pleased they were,
How arrogant of humanity to clap an animal for clapping.
I didn't enjoy the 12:30 show.
Or the 16:30 show.
Or the next morning's 12:30 show.

Poem #113

The zoo was full of children pointing,

"Look mum," they would say as they pointed.

Dutifully the mother would turn, already knowing the script she should adopt,

Regardless of what should face her.

"Look mum, a wolf," the children screamed in excitement,

Pointing at a clump of fur sleeping in the sun that could quite easily have been a shag carpet.

"Ah yeah, a wolf," she said turning away ready to stare into another window and repeat the same thing all over again.

This could be a wolf!

Poem #15

There was a farm in the zoo,
Like one with horses, cows and sheep.
I felt cheated,
I saw all those animals on the way to the zoo.
Sure, there were ducks,
But I've seen ducks.

I turned to my wife,
Who like a chump,
Was absolutely loving the goats.

Ryan Kenny

Poem #72

The zoo opened at 10am,
Someone should have told the fucking animals that.

Poem #86

A crowd had gathered around the lion enclosure,
I recognised some of them from the sea lion show, so I wasn't
holding out much hope for anything impressive.
But I was wrong,
I was so wrong.
Anjan Hi Way has his cock out.

Fathers turned to mothers in amazement,
Children asked questions to no-one in particular.
Young boys sniggered,
Old men sniggered.
 Anjan Hi Way was a sight to behold,
A spectacular enough attraction that it even had its own
diagram on the map.

A voice echoed over the tanoy,

"And he we have Anjan Hi Way, the only elephant with a
Prince Albert piecing."

Ryan Kenny

Poem #109

A congregation of alligators,
A cauldron of bats,
A gang of buffalo.
A coalition of cheetahs
A caravan of camels,
A pod of dolphins.
A flamboyance of flamingos,
A business of ferrets,
A raft of otters.
A conspiracy of lemurs,
A tower of giraffes,

One tasty soup.

Poem #7

There is a Komodo dragon at every single Zoo I've ever been too,

"There are very few Komodo dragons left in the wild," the plaque would say.

Of course, there is,

They are all fucking about in small towns across Britain.

Poem #20

Thirty children ran amok,
Hi-Vis vests flapping in the wind.
Three teachers working by the clock,
Reporting on the teaching assistant who'd been limbed.

Clip boards clattered to the ground,
Unaccomplished work sheets in the mud.
Screaming, shouting, every kind of sound,
Teaching assistant covered in blood.

Its four o'clock, head count, ready for the bus,
Making sure all the children are there, including Ryan.
What an average day for all that fuss,
Apart from when the teaching assistant was attacked by a
Lion.

Poem #142

A cackle of hyenas,
A richness of martens,
A cete of badgers.

A shadow of jaguars,
A leap of leopards,
A labour of moles.

A prickle of porcupines,
A span of mules,
A scurry of Squirrels.

One tasty pie.

Ryan Kenny
Poem #34

A pack of wolves,
A pod of whales,
A streak of tigers.

A crash of rhinos,
A colony of rabbits,
A turmoil of porpoises.

A drift of pigs,
A troop of monkeys,
A bloat of hippos.

One tired format.

Some Words, In an Order, On a Page.

Chapters 13-16.

I have decided to group these three chapters together. I find the book reads much easier when these chapters are joined.

I found Alan Titchmarsh's book a difficult read and I personally feel had he combined his chapters into one more manageable chapter then it would have flowed easier. I did send this recommendation to his agent, and I can only assume future prints of Alan Titchmarsh: How to Garden: Small Gardens, would heed my advice.

I took the liberty in seeing whether members of the public and fellow followers of Alan's work had similar views but I could only find this one-star review:

What is your definition of small?

Those looking for help with a small garden might like to know that the definition used in this book is a garden "that is no larger than a tennis court."

Unfortunately, I need help with a SMALL garden!

<u>Poem #29</u>

It was springtime,

The flowers were in an almighty bloom.

David and his wife Sally roasted a freshly caught rabbit over a spit.

"Did you remove all the missing pet posters off all the lamppost David?" Sally said pulling away some singeing fur.

"Posters?" David chuckled. "Don't you mean the specials boards?"

They both laughed heartily.

As Thumper burnt.

And a child wept somewhere.

Ryan Kenny

Poem #99

Tony spent all summer inside.

In fact, he had spent the last four summers inside.

His parents were originally worried for him.

But he shouldn't have stolen that Toyota Yaris four years ago.

Poem #127

Leaves are weird.

They spend all year,
Growing.

Only to turn wrinkled,
And crumpled under,
Feet.

In some ways I,
Suppose
We are a lot like,
Leaves.

Eventually on the ground, rotting and forgotten about,
But leaves grow again and new life blooms.

Ryan Kenny
Poem #102

Christmas was cancelled.
Effigies of Santa were burnt in the streets,
People asked for answers.
Demanded them.

Parents, sick and tired of the glory going towards that sick man,
Rubbed their hands together at the thought of appreciation they were now to receive.

Yeah, naturally Santa had his defenders,
Those within his inner arctic circle.
But it was not enough,
The power of the people was too great.

Santa looked on from his hotel room,
Thousands screamed for justice below.
He picked the last piece of mince pie out of his beard,
How he wished he had had never said those things on Twitter all those years ago.

Some Words, In an Order, On a Page.

Chapter 17: The Phantom Chapter

I've always written poetry. Writing is very cathartic. The thought of someone reading and thinking the words I have vomited on to the page is oddly satisfying,

Like now, you are saying my words in your head.

I am officially in your head.

You are desperate for a wee aren't you. You weren't before but reading this now is making you think that it might be safer to go.

Put the book down for a moment and go.

Seriously go.

"I don't need to go, get on with poetry," you are saying to yourself. Literally you are saying this to yourself in your head. Madness

Now go for a piss and stop having this mild crisis of self.

See you soon for more poems.

Poem #148

There was a flood in the Bachelors soup factory,

It should have been a serious incident, but the fire crews and other general emergency services couldn't contain their joy at the scene.

The river burst into the powder stores,

Minestrone seeped through the floors,

Mushrooms expanded and forced open the safety doors.

Two women, bobbed around on top of a giant crouton,

Their boss wasn't as lucky though as he was found drowned and trapped beneath a lump of chunky chicken.

Fourteen people died at the flood in the Bachelors soup factory,

But it still earnt its place as the funniest flood this century.

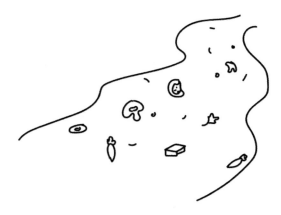

Poem #78

(This poem was written using only the first word on the first page proper of every book on my bookshelf)

Aardvark,
Aardvark,
A,
Aardvark,
Aardvark.
It,
It,
It,
It,
It,
Aardvark.

Poem #97

I looked at my bookshelf,
And questioned my previous purchases,
But sometimes you just can never remember if you already owned that book.
Dictionary,
Dictionary,
An old dictionary,
Dictionary,
Dictionary.
1984
1984: Abridged
1984: Unabridged
1984: School Edition
1984: School Edition (I moved schools mid GCSE)
My favourite animals by Edwina Curry.

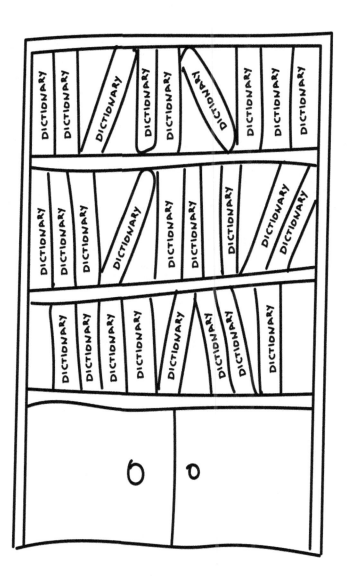

Poem #130

The Jury pondered,
Scratching their heads,
There was just something about the defendant that oozed guilt.
It could have been the way he walked,
Perhaps it was how he carried himself,
Maybe it was the wry smile,
The crooked tie,
Or maybe it was because his prints were all over the victim's body.

Ryan Kenny

Poem #118

Mike Dean placed his whistle into his salivating mouth,
Taking comfort from the smooth metallic taste.
75,000 people,
In the so called 'theatre of dreams',
Berated him with obscenities too crass to print.
He had never asked for any of this,
He had always wanted to be an accountant.
But he had filled in the work experience sheet in wrong,
And one thing led to another,
He could never build up the courage to say.

<u>Poem #50</u>

Anne caused a stir when she had arrived at the knitting group without her personalised needles.

She went to borrow some off her friend, Maureen.

"Hands off my things!" Maureen yelled as she stabbed Anne in the eye with a needle etched with the name Maureen.

Anne was rushed to A&E,

She reached into her pocket for her phone so that she may call her daughters.

As she fiddled between the boiled sweets and used tissues she felt the cold metal of her own needles,

"What a palaver," she thought, unnecessarily blind.

Ryan Kenny
<u>Poem #25</u>

I went to the chippy,
"Just waiting for chips," the chef shouted merrily.
In a chippy.
I understood that I had to wait for fish, battered sausage or
even a pea fritter,
But chips…
Me and four fellow chip desirers were stuck in chippy limbo,
Our hungry skin cold against the greasy walls.
Unsuspecting chumps walk in,
We must explain our state of purgatory.
The cycle continues, the chumps become one of us.
All waiting for that sweet release of a large chips.
We smile as we take the warm white bag, knowing we had
been treated like fools, but also aware that we will be leaning up
against the wall same time next Friday.

Poem #88

Karl,
Despite his A-Level in general studies,
Discovered trough terrible research,
That broken glass,
Tastes exactly like blood.

Poem #124

I'm not very good at writing similes,
It's like,
You know,
Like...

Poem #141

Roger put down his HB pencil and stared at the masterpiece he had just created.

In a moment of sudden turmoil, he reached into his brown slacks and glided his member over the pages.

Urine gushed out,

Destroying his words in a beautiful way.

But that was fine, the world simply wasn't ready for his sensual Good Morning Britain fanfiction.

Poem #138

The Gudmundsson family had been collecting Weetabix flakes for over five years.

Brian, the dad, would rinse the bowls over a sieve and freeze dry the remains.

Lucy, the mum, would hoover the bottom of the box and squish together the Weetabix dust.

The children, both nine years old, would steal crumbs off the table during breakfast club.

There was a hope that eventually they could make their own Weetabix from the collected bits and finally take on the giants of the cereal world.

Sixty months and a divorce later they had only managed to form 20 GudmundssonBix.

What a waste of time.

Poem #103

"Ewww, that's disgusting," Karen said as Claude did one of his little poo's on the desk. (It was about the size of the average snail.)

He turned to Karen, rolled his eyes, and slithered back into his seat.

Lord Sugar would be back soon,

The wait was thrilling.

And as per usual, he would blame it on one of the unsuspecting project managers.

<u>Poem #94</u>

The farmer laughed to himself,
The naive boy had sold him a magic cow for some beans.
He rushed home,
Planted the cow…

Nothing happened.

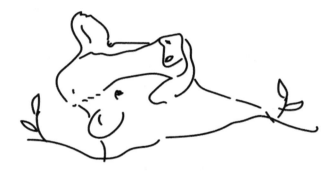

Chapter 18: The Attack of The Chapters

We are now many poems into the book, and I understand that you may need a break. Considering this information, I have decided to throw a bunch of interesting facts about resting and sleep.

- Our minds incorporate sounds and smells around us when we're dreaming. If you're napping while someone's cooking lasagne, you might start dreaming you're dining at an Italian restaurant.

- Humans are the only mammal that willingly delays sleep.

- If you live to be 75 years old, you'll have spent approximately 25 years sleep – 6 of those years will be jam-packed with dreams.

- More than 80% of people under 30 dream in colour but just over 10% of people dream entirely in black and white their whole lives.

Poem #131

The game of Cluedo had gotten out of hand,
Mum was searching in the shed for some lead piping,
Dad was ushering Grandma into other rooms.
All whilst Uncle Mike lay dying on the floor begging for one
of them to call the ambulance.

<u>Poem #107</u>

The game of monopoly had gotten out of hand,
Mum was taking rent off all those who stepped into the lounge,
Dad was ushering Grandma into a makeshift jail.
All whilst Uncle Mike lay breathless, trying to be resuscitated by paramedics.

Poem #4

The game of mousetrap had gotten out of hand,
Mum was watching endless TikTok's about Rube Goldberg machines,
Dad was trying to position Grandma ever so carefully above the bath.
All whist Uncle Mike's wake carried on around them.

Ryan Kenny

Poem #39

Edward was on a date.

He had dressed smart and had even found time to wash his pits.

Edward smiled when he saw the table,

He dreamed of seeing his date lay upon it.

It was cold,

White,

And slabbish.

The morgue was lonely sometimes.

Poem #111

Barbara moaned in pleasure,
She shook in pure delight.
It was the perfect fit,
Everything felt just right.
The moment it slotted in,
And it all disappeared from sight. *

*An ode to the best Tetris piece, the long thin blue one.

Poem #59

"WHATS THE MATTER WITH YOU NOW!" Eli yelled.
But Karl didn't answer,
As he had been dead for hours.

Ryan Kenny

<u>Poem #143</u>

Kyle booked himself a hotel room,
Nothing cheap but nothing Holiday Inn standard.
He bought himself a UV light,
Just to double check,
That he was still covered in semen.

He couldn't get to sleep otherwise.

Poem #125

Peter had been sat in Steve's house for 40 minutes and he still didn't know the Wi-Fi password.

Steve was a very poor host,

So naturally Peter killed him.

But had no idea how to dispose of the body as he still couldn't to the Wi-Fi.

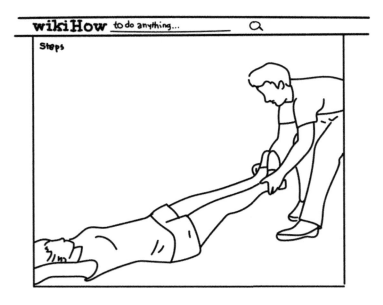

Poem #16

This is the ballad of Gregory Wimble.
He was a simple man with simple dreams.

Gregory Wimble lived in an ordinary town,
He worked an ordinary job (IT or admin I imagine),
He drove home in his ordinary car, to his ordinary house to greet his ordinary wife.

But Gregory Wimble was no ordinary man.

Gregory Wimble had one leg that was 2 metres longer than the other.

Some Words, In an Order, On a Page.

Chapter 19: The Revenge of the Chapter.

I am currently sat in a library.

I have a bottle of Vimto beside me which I bought from Poundland.

The bottle has £1.09 on the label.

And I bought it for 75p.

So please forgive me if this chapter comes across in any way erratic or chaotic because right now, I have no idea what to think.

Poem #93

She wanted to dance,
Oh, how she wanted to dance.
Blood scattered across the walls,
Revellers screaming.
But still she 'grooved',
Stepping over the bodies as she did.
The club was chaos,
DJ, Molotov in-hand grinned.

But still,

Sophie Elis-Bextor danced.

Ryan Kenny

<u>Poem #68</u>

Fake taxi.

Woke up in the morning like I do all the time,
Had to be at the station by quarter-past nine.
Wave down a cab as anyone would do,
When a car calling itself a Taxi passes you.
A man and a woman smile on their face,
Opened the door and plonked me in place.
I said,
"Don't worry sir I'll get another,"
He said,
"Whilst you're in here mate, you're my step-brother."
So, I sat in the corner, trying not to cry,
Those two went at it, thigh slapping thigh.
They finished with a moan and a roar,
He pattered my shoulder and opened the door.
It was half 12, three hours late for work,
"15 quid mate, pay up, don't be a jerk."
So, I gave them my cash like a sad little mouse,
Turned around,
They left,
I was still at my house.

<u>Poem #45</u>

A comedian/poet/author/great lover sat in the library.
He was writing his very best work,
And then the computer cra

Poem #101

Malcom saw the light getting closer,
He was scared,
There was nothing he could do.
The cold metal struck him in the face,
His nose bled,
His eyes wept.
Malcolm had dropped his own phone on his face as he lay in
bed.

Prick.

Poem #70

Stacey went bowling,
It took her ages to find the right ball.
She searched all eighteen lanes,
She carefully studied each grubby ball.
Finally, she found one.
The weight was fine, but her fingers kept getting lodged in the
sweaty holes.
Instead of admitting that she had chubby little man fingers,
She bowled anyway,
Severely snapping her wrist in three places.

Poem #23

For years men and
have drawn them.
of immaturity or
write what you
to wonder how
have them etched
reckon 40% of all
a thought. However

immature folk alike
I suppose it's a sign
maybe it's a case of
know. I often tend
many schoolbooks
onto the fabrics. I
graffiti is penis. Just
, rest assured that

This author is
not the kind of
immature
person to do
such a thing.
It's a childish
thing to do.
Also, the
pictures are
never truly
accurate and

I strive for
accuracy with my
work.

Poem #139

Jennifer had accidently put on a high-vis jacket on the way to work,

Though she noticed that people began to take her more seriously.

No longer would people stare at her with eyes full of fear,

The high-vis seems to give her an air of authority that Jennifer loved.

It was only yesterday that a group of three students vomited by her feet when they saw her,

There was no vomit this day.

There were loads of questions rushing through her mind.

Should she buy her own jacket?

Is orange the best high-vis colour?

And what was she going to do were her old coat now?

It took her ages to sew together all that fresh human skin.

Ryan Kenny

Poem #119

The rolling stones were in town,
All the hotels and inns were completely full,
Which absolutely destroyed Mary and Joseph's birthing plan.

Some Words, In an Order, On a Page.

Chapter 20: Politics

It may be clear from my work that I tend to stay well away from politics. However, it had become clear that it is my job as an author to comment on the clusterfuck that is the current world political landscape.

So, with all that in mind I have decided to collate all my vaguely political poems into one chapter.

To get you in the mood for politics I have included the election results from the 1997 general election. The constituency below is that of Orkney and Shetland.

Liberal Democrats: Jim Wallace   52%

Labour: James Paton   18.3%

SNP: Willie Ross   12.7%

Conservative: Hope Anderson 12.2%

Referendum: Francis Adamson4%

Natural Law: Christian Wharton   0.6%

Independent: Arthur Robertson   0.3%

Turnout 20,665   Liberal Democrats hold.

Poem #31

"Order order!" The speaker screamed from his massive chair.
But it was no use,
Chaos had taken over and even he and the powers given to
him were not enough to quash it.
One MP, probably a minister for sport, threw a shotput over
to the other side,
Whilst another began ripping up the green seats and
whacking their opponents with them.
The Brexit minister tried to leave,
The shadow minister for the treasury started to pick pockets.
Most though, were scrapping on the floor inside massive
cartoon dust clouds.
In all the foray they had gotten mixed up.
Some were no longer on their given side of the house.
Confusion started to dominate the faces of the MP's,
They didn't know what to think,
They had been too busy attacking each other to actually
remember why they were there in the first place.

But then a man with a big bag of money waltzed in,
And fighting continued.

Poem #106

Titus Pontius looked at his sundial,

"Fuck!"

He checked his calendar on the off chance he had booked a holiday,

15th March,

"FUCK!" He shouted again when he realised that not only was he not on holiday, but he was on the emperor bodyguard duty.

He strapped on his sandals and rushed into the kitchen area to give his mother a kiss on the cheek.

"Oh, hey sweetie," she said with a typical mothers smile on her face, "don't rush off now, I've made you breakfast.'"

"But mother, I am late for my duty and the emperor has a massive speech today".

"Don't you worry about that, your bread is getting mouldy, eat it up now, and besides, Emperor Caesar is surrounded by his best friends, all will be fine."

"Yeah, I suppose," Titus muttered with a mouth full of bread.

Poem #66

After many years have slipped by, the leaders of the Greeks,
Opposed by the Fates, and damaged by the war,
Build a horse of mountainous size, through Pallas's divine art,
And weave planks of fir over its ribs,
They pretend it's a votive offering: this rumour spreads.
They secretly hide a picked body of men, chosen by lot,
There, in the dark body, filling the belly and the huge
cavernous insides with armed warriors.

The city of Troy was ever so thankful for their gift,
So, they burnt it as an offering to the Gods.

"Wow, it's amazing how the burning wood smells so meaty,"
Priam said ready for a peaceful night sleep.

Ryan Kenny

Poem #14

A sceptical iguana sat on his rock,
He had been somewhat ousted from his community for his radical thoughts.
His time in isolation however just made his beliefs stronger,
His iguana brain could not believe how not one member of his tree clan could see it.
He looked at the Iguana King,
And the Iguana Queen,
And those high up in his society.
He was absolutely convinced,
That they were humans.

<u>Poem #146</u>

The Question Time audience shuffled out of the studio,
Sunlight burning their skin.
Some crawled to the local library to see if their friends had created yet another viral clip,
Whilst others, the more organised of the bunch, checked the train times for next Thursday.
None of them spoke,
The spell was strong,
Only Fiona Bruce could release them.
The trapped noticed how the freed were no longer with them,
To be chosen by Fiona meant freedom.
Erik had been an audience member for forty-two years, one arm muscled beyond belief from his desperate attempt to ask a question and buy his life back,
But Erik would never be chosen.
Dimbleby had made that quite clear.

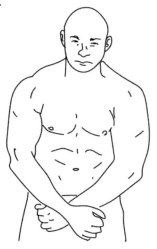

Poem #5

Harold Wilson, Edward Heath, John Major, Tony Blair,
Margaret Thatcher, Winston Churchill, Alec Douglas-Home,
Clement Attlee, Stanley Baldwin, Bonar Law, Lord John
Russell,
Robert Peel, William Lamb, William Gladstone,
Disraeli, Johnson, Gordon Brown, Chamberlain
Liz Truss, Theresa May, and "The Catcher in the Rye",
Robert Walpole, Lloyd-George, Robert Gascoyne-Cecil,
Spencer Compton, Henry Pelham, William Pit, goodbye.

We didn't start the fire
It was always burning, since the world's been turning.

BUT WE HAVE ALL CONTRIBUTED TO IT.

Poem #71

Boris Johnson
OrisJ Ohnsonb
Risjo Hnsonbo
Isjoh Nsonbor
Sjohn Sonbori
Johns Onboris

"Get off me"! Boris screamed to John.

Ohnso NborisJ
Hnson BorisJo
Nsonb OrisJoh
Sonbo Risjohn
Onbor Isjohns
Nbori Sjohnso
Boris Johnson

"Thankyou"' Boris said for the first time as John Major found somewhere else to sit. *

*I have no idea what this is either.

Chapter 21: Palette Cleanse

I think it is clear after all that political satire we need a few more whimsical additions to this anthology.

So, this within this chapter I will try and bring the whimsy. I have no idea what I am going to do yet. I am sure there will be a few bangers in here that make you sniff in laughter. There is also a high chance that one or two of the following poems will bring no emotion out of you.

It is fine to not feel emotion whilst reading my poems.

I feel no emotion writing them.

It is also acceptable to express any of these emotions whilst trying to decipher the meaning behind my words:

-Desiderium
-Compunctious
-Alexithymia
-Leucocholy
-Compathy
-Callosity

<u>Poem #28</u>

Three frogs lined up on their individual lily pads ready to cross their river,

Three other frogs, on the other side, were already trying to cross though.

They stared at each other,

No one wanted to make the first move.

A flurry of young mathematicians watched keenly from the bank,

All debating how the frogs could get to the other side without sharing a lily pad.

Upon seeing this, all six frogs made a pact,

And they just swam across the river,

Because they are frogs.

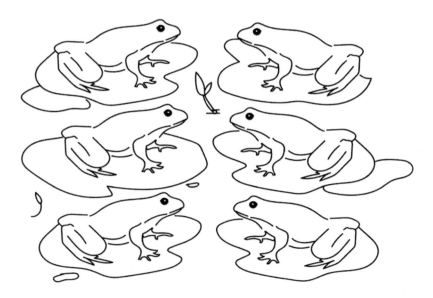

Poem #22

The celebrity had grown accustomed to their mask,
Life was much easier in his giant courgette costume.
Sure, he would have to unmask at the end of the season,
But in the meantime, he applied for as many roles as he could
as courgette.
The judges thought he was either Anthony Joshua, Kate
Garraway, that guy who sits with his sister on Gogglebox or
David Attenborough,
They were all wrong.
For he was Courgette,
He will always be Courgette.

Poem #132

Ted held his chest,
The rest of the gymnastics team continued to cartwheel regardless.
They had seen it all before,
Ted would be fine soon,
He would just blame his Achilles heart again.

Poem # 92

Tony was assured by the vendor that his new hat was great,
Why would the vendor lie?
Strangers shrivelled their faces when Tony came close,
That never happened before he bought the hat.
The vendor was an honest man,
Only honest men can run businesses, surely.
Tony looked in the mirror,
Sure, the hat was made of asbestos,
And it was far too heavy for one head to hold without it
crushing the neck below.
Of course, some people would object to the smiling picture of
Josip Broz Tito adorning it,
And the fact it squeaked as he walked.
But Tony loved it,
And Tony would not listen to public opinion.

One man said it was good and that was enough for him.

Poem #35

I
Am
A big
Angry
Mountain.
Some say I am
Dormant but I prefer
To use the word: resting.
Just use your little human brain
And imagine how much rest you'll
Need if you ejaculated boiling hot lava.
Thought so. Now have a bit more sympathy.
I bet your ejaculate doesn't have the power to level
Entire populations or even block out the earth's light.
Let me rest, stop counting the days, cos it makes me horny

Ryan Kenny

Poem #10

People screamed,
But Lucy still moshed.
Lucy was a typical mosher,
She would mosh until all the moshing was done.
The others called her a moshie because wherever she went in
life she would behave quite moshy.
She would mosh on the bus,
At the tax office,
Under the stairs too.
"Stop all this moshing," the security lady pleaded,
"Never!" Lucy said moshingly.

Lucy had lost all her friends,
Her family no longer spoke to her,
And hadn't had a stable relationship since the great '08 mosh
pit at the Cliff Richard concert.

She really needed help,
But just kept pushing people away.

She died alone at the age of 32,
Moshed right into some barbed wire she did.

Poem #121

He tried eight rotations to the left,
Then another seven to the right.
Only mere seconds ago did he release a sheet of toilet paper
from its circular sheath,
But now it alluded him.
His fingers scraped at the edges to find the 'end', but it was
gone,
Hidden from sight and touch.
He took a deep breath,
Felt the desperate need to wipe,
And attacked the paper once more.

Ryan Kenny
Poem #122

He stood in fear as he washed his hands,

A boiling stream of hot water trickling over the millilitre of soap that the machine had allowed him.

Someone in the far cubicle was struggling,

They were banging at the walls and cursing their very existence.

He had felt that man's pain before,

They were being denied the very right to wipe.

He felt himself about to speak,

To offer the poor soul aid,

But his mouth went dry.

This was the men's bathroom,

You do NOT talk to each other in the men's bathroom,

It was everyman for themselves.

Poem #123

Armitage Shanks laughed from the other cubicle,
He had caused the chaos.
He was looking at one of his designs,
The perfect infuriation tools.

Armitage Shanks had designed a toilet roll dispenser that at random would lock its roll,
No matter how much the roll would spin the paper became impossible to obtain.

He heard someone about to help,
But silencing themselves just in time to obey the unwritten laws of the men's bathroom.
Armitage imagined the struggling man's hand bent backwards the hole purposely designed to be too small,
His wrists lacerated on the unnecessary teeth of the dispenser.

Armitage Shanks wanted chaos,
He thrived on chaos.
"BOW DOWN TO SHANKS!" He laughed from his cubicle.

Ryan Kenny

Poem #69

Hehe hehe hehe hehe hehe hehe hehe hehe hehe hehe hehe
Hehe   hehe   hehe
Hehe   hehe   hehe
Hehe   hehe   hehe
Hehe hehe hehe hehe   hehe

Haha   haha haha haha haha
Haha   haha   haha
Haha   haha   haha
Haha   haha   haha
Haha haha haha haha haha haha hahahaha haha hahahaha.

Some Words, In an Order, On a Page.

Chapter 22: The cut.

The poems in this chapter are a collection of poems that didn't make the cut for the book. I had to cut a few poems for a variety of reasons. Sometimes the poem was too far beyond the comprehension of the human mind and in other instances it was just a pile of dog dirt.

I will leave you to decide whether the following poems are the former or latter, but I think we can all be safe in the knowledge that they didn't make the cut for the book.

Poem #32

The author was sat in the library,
A man was playing on a computer to his left and to his right a lady tried to book her theory test.

He wondered if they had any idea of the masterpiece being created between them both.

Probably not, the chess player had just shown his lack of awareness by bringing his knight to D6 and thus leaving a clear pathway for his opponent to attack with a Queen/Rook combo.

The author sipped on his Ribena from the pound shop,
It only cost him 75p,

And his sanity.

Ryan Kenny

Poem #104

A baby group sung nursery rhymes at the back of the room,

They started on the classics like Baa Baa and Incy Wincy but then began to branch out.

They followed The Wheels on The Bus with a terrific rendition of Stairway to Heaven before belting out a tremendous cover of Bob Dylan's Hurricane.

The whole library was on their feet,

Three librarians, two sullen customers and a sweet lady packing away the mugs from the tea lunch.

They treated the standing ovation as a silent encore,

So finished with a cheeky cover of Bring Me to Life by Evanescence.

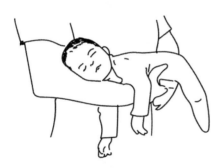

Poem #49

They had added yet another Egghead to the roster,
Bringing the total to 67.
Despite the program being around fifty years old,
Chris, (The one who I genuinely thought the show was named for) was still on the team, constantly answering questions on music.
A plaque had been installed under the desk in memory of the original team,
Kevin, may he rest in peace,
Was being controlled by two of the newest members in a sort of Weekend at Bernie's situation.

The challengers won,
Ending the Egghead's 239th straight victory. *

*I wrote this whilst watching Eggheads, can you tell?

Ryan Kenny
Poem #52

An army of frogs,
A bale of turtles,
A colony of ants.

A shoal of bass,
A sounder of boar,
A sedge of cranes.

A rag of colts,
A bed of clams,
A peep of chickens.

A dule of doves,
A parade of elephants,
A skulk of foxes.

A charm of finches,
A charm of goldfinches
A cloud of grasshoppers.

One unorganised ark.

Some Words, In an Order, On a Page.

Chapter 23: Poems for the audience.

Now, not only am I a gifted wordsmith but I am also a wonderful performer. In these performances I often write a poem for the audience.

This chapter will only make sense if you were in any of those very selective small crowds

However, there seems to be rise in popularity of #outofcontext so I like the little capitalist whore I am, am obviously going to jump on that trend.

Yeah, maybe I should set the scene before each poem but why should I, Tolkien never sets the scene in his work. You can just imagine the characters in the crowd and see what kind of high jinks they got up to.

So welcome to Out of Context Poems.

Poem #55

Oh Tommy,
Phone call from Mommy.
(a lot of these audience poems rhyme, I know, YUCK.)
Six comedians,
We spend years developing our acts,
Yet you are the funniest here,
You legendary T**T.

Manchester 03/02/2022

Poem #19

Aaron works in telecoms,
Diane works until he cums.

Manchester 08/07/22

Poem #9

I have always wanted to gig in front of minesweeper,
You were fucking, now you are not, Alex is no Keeper.
I am alright at comedy my dad can vouch,
John, you forgot to take home your casting couch.

Leeds 20/09/21

Poem #95

Sean, Liam and Dave on the rails takes its toll,
Other Sean lubing up the pole.
Look at me, look at me, turning over the page,
You two that work here,
Get of your phones,
Check that guys I.D,
He is clearly underage.

Doncaster 01/09/21

Poem #134

The energetic audience loved the MC,
Especially the carrot loving salesman Andy.
Four months of engagement, love like bird song,
Judging by his cool job and her not so good one, it's not going
to last long.

Manchester 26/08/21

Poem #43

Aldi Gareth Bale stood at the bar,
A microphone you can't hear from afar,
Less seats in here than a Reliant Robin car,
Wish I was back home,
Crying myself to sleep,
In Manchestar.

Mold 10/08/21

Poem #144

Jenny from the block,
Invest in a clock.
Booking dot Yeah,
Booking dot NO!
I'm taking my custom to Trivago.

Liverpool 03/04/22

Poem #135

I've got more confidence than a pissed baker,
More brains than Tom the inbetweener.
I get much more loving than the lying matchmaker,
My name is Paul,
And I am,
A note taker.

Sheffield, 06/06/22

Some Words, In an Order, On a Page.

Chapter 24: The penultimate chapter.

Well, it is almost over. It has been one hell of a ride. As a reward to you I will give you this story.

I used to be a semi-professional dancer but due to an injury I had to give that up and take up a job in a large supermarket, which incidentally was right next to a concert hall. I could never let my old profession go so I was allowed to wear my old leotard on the shop floor. I personally think that is because my tiny stature meant the supermarket didn't have any uniform that fit me, but I didn't complain.

On my first day, we were expecting a very busy evening as Elton John was performing in the neighbouring building. It was during his very short UK tour titled Spice.

What I didn't quite expect was the man himself to walk into the shop.

Due to my passion for dancing and obvious love of Elton I was given the job of being his personal shopper. It was amazing. But he insisted on not using a basket. For his tour he needed a bunch of ingredients. He grabbed the nutmeg, the cardamom, the saffron and the ginger. But he needed my help, so he said.

"Hold me cloves sir tiny dancer."

Poem #115

The Peterson family was all ready for their holidays.
They had packed everything.

The sun cream: Factor 50+
The important documents: Walleted
The plants: In the sink
The shorts: Long and cargo
And the Lilo: Inflated
Which was a fucking nightmare to pack.

Ryan Kenny

Poem #67

David Attenborough took out a matchbox from his top pocket,
It was tattered and perhaps older than he is.
He gently pushed one finger in one end,
Opening a gap that was small enough for him to peak through.
He smiled and giggled like a 6-year-old with a plastic triceratops,
And pulled out, by its tail, a tiny mouse.
He unlocked his jaw and swallowed the creature whole,
The rest of the restaurant looked at his aghast.
But David was a national treasure,
And could get away with that kind of tomfoolery.

Poem #37

This does sort of scan,
But I can promise you this,
Is not a Haiku.

Ryan Kenny
Poem #90

Neil refused to look at the menu,

He pointed at the cobweb covered specials board and nodded.

The waiter looked to the chef, his tall white hat growing even taller above raised eyebrows.

The chef rang his father, the original owner of the establishment, and jotted down notes with an alarming speed.

Neil prepared himself, releasing a personal soup spoon from a velvet sheath.

He noted the waiters all gossiping about him, their burnt fingers pointing at his table,

He stood,

On the table,

And wrapped a bib round his neck, the words 'I'm a special boy' sewn into it with golden thread.

Eventually a steaming hot minestrone soup was placed in front of him,

Neil looked at it, looked at his spoon and then at the closest waiter,

"Sorry I'm Vegan."

Poem #47

This poem holds important information about the creation of the new world order.

The Illuminate ███████ is ████

real,

and

your favourite

Teacher, is ██.

deep,

within

it,

sorry.

*Poem redacted due to security concerns.

<u>Poem #12</u>

A busy Tate Modern was teaming with people pretending to understand art,

Suddenly, eight well-meaning citizens ripped off their turtlenecks to reveal bright yellow T-Shirts that had the words 'Cars be bad' printed upon them.

They reached into their bags and pulled out a seemingly endless amount of Philadelphia original.

The security was in panic mode,

But were too late,

Various flavours of soft cheese had been smeared across the walls.

The curator rushed down from his office,

And demanded all people be removed from the floor.

He pulled out a string and began cordoning off the lumpy white walls,

He was erect, at full length,

He whispered to himself erotically,

"Art."

A plaque was made, and thousands of tickets sold.

It began to smell.

Art.

Poem #11

Three cats sat in the cinema,
"This is shit," one cat meowed to the other.
Andrew Lloyd Webber cried in the corner,
His tears filtering through the guttering on his face. (Wrinkles)

He tossed his James Cordon hoody in the nearest bin and spat
at a picture of Judi Dench, Dame Judi Dench,
How could she do this to him?

But then the cats purred at Jason Derulo, and all was forgiven.

Ryan Kenny

Some Words, In an Order, On a Page.

The Final Chapter

We have reached the final chapter and for that we need to give ourselves a pat on the back or a cheeky smack on the bum.

Enjoy these last 5 poems.
Or not.
It makes no difference to me*

*It actually makes a lot of difference to me; my day can be ruined by any negative feedback**

** I could be having the best day with Weetabix in the morning and Roller Coaster Tycoon in the evening. But if someone says I am not very good at a thing, I will crumble. ***

*** Please review this book.

Poem #117

"My mum says you are what you eat,"

"So, if you eat runner beans, you'll be come a runner?"

"Yep,"

"And if you eat French fries, you'll become French?"

"Yep,"

"And if you eat, what's this then?"

"Its Green Giant sweetcorn,"

"Green Giant?" They both ate their sweetcorn.
The mom came rushing in as the screams began.
"No, No, what are you doing, stop eating th...."
But the boys did not stop.
They grew and grew.
Breaking through the newly plastered ceiling and into the loft conversation.
"Mom, what do we do, it hurts!" One of the boys said in a booming voice. But it was too late.

Ryan Kenny

<u>Poem #27</u>

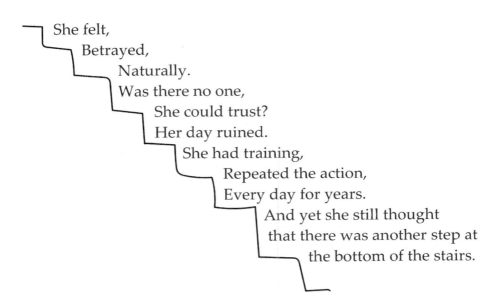

She felt,
 Betrayed,
  Naturally.
 Was there no one,
  She could trust?
 Her day ruined.
  She had training,
   Repeated the action,
   Every day for years.
    And yet she still thought
    that there was another step at
     the bottom of the stairs.

Poem #54

Travis got spunk all in his eye,
He cried uncontrollably.
His skin was itchy,
Throat dry.
He felt weak,
No matter where he went, spunk filled the air.
He was a strong human and yet simple tasks would become
impossible because of the thick mist of spunk.
Travis should have listened when even the BBC had warned
that there was a high spunk count.
But the grass needed cutting,
So, he bravely took his antihistamine,
And prayed the flowers and plants were feeling less horny.

Poem #150

It's strange,
I haven't met you yet,
But I know you are perfect,
It's odd,
I haven't held your hand,
But I know, I would never let it go.
It's bizarre,
I have no idea what colour your eyes will be,
But I know, deep within, they will only see love from me.
It's weird,
I haven't got much myself,
But I know, I will give it all to you.
Its mad,
I haven't at any point felt without,
But I know, you are the filling to the gap in my heart that I never knew I had.
It's strange.

Love from Daddy

Printed in Great Britain
by Amazon

31070115R00118